The Quotation Bank for A-Level

A Doll's House

Henrik Ibsen

Copyright © 2023 Esse Publishing Limited and Mary Hind-Portley
The moral rights of the authors have been asserted.

First published in 2023 by:
The Quotation Bank
Esse Publishing Limited
10 9 8 7 6 5 4 3 2 1

All rights reserved. No part of this publication may be reproduced, resold, stored in a retrieval system or transmitted in any form, or by any means (electronic, photocopying, mechanical or otherwise) without the prior written permission of both the copyright owners and the publisher.

A CIP catalogue record for this book is available from the British Library.
ISBN 978-1-7396080-0-2

All enquiries to: contact@thequotationbank.co.uk
Every effort has been made to trace and contact all relevant copyright holders. However, if contacted the publisher will rectify any omission or error at the earliest opportunity.

Printed and bound by Target Print Limited, Broad Lane, Cottenham, Cambridge CB24 8SW.

www.thequotationbank.co.uk

Introduction

How The Quotation Bank can help you in your exams   4
How to use The Quotation Bank   5

Quotations

Act One   6
Act Two   15
Act Three   22
Critical and Contextual Quotations   31

Revision and Essay Planning

Performance History   41
How to revise effectively   42
Suggested revision activities   43
Glossary   44

Welcome to The Quotation Bank, the comprehensive guide to all the key quotations you need to succeed in your exams.

Whilst you may have read the play, watched a film adaptation, understood the plot and have a strong grasp of context, all questions in your A-Levels require you to write a focused essay, full of textual references and quotations (be they textual, critical or contextual), and most importantly, quotations that you then analyse.

I think we all agree it is *analysis* that is the tricky part – and that is why we are here to help!

The Quotation Bank takes 25 of the most important quotations from the text, interprets them, analyses them, highlights literary and dramatic techniques Ibsen has used, puts them in context, and suggests which quotations you might use in which essays. We have also included 10 contextual and critical quotations, analysed them, and linked them closely to the text, all for you to explore.

At the end of **The Quotation Bank** we have put together a performance history and great revision exercises to help you prepare for your exam. We have also included a detailed glossary to make sure you completely understand what certain literary terms actually mean!

How The Quotation Bank can help you in your exams.

The Quotation Bank is designed to make sure every point you make in an essay clearly fulfils the Assessment Objectives an examiner will be using when marking your work.

Every quotation comes with the following detailed material:

Interpretation: The interpretation of each quotation allows you to fulfil **AO1**, articulating an informed, personal response, and **AO5**, using different interpretations to inform your exploration of the text.

Techniques: Using associated concepts and terminology (in this case, the techniques used by Ibsen) is a key part of **AO1**, and can help you identify and analyse ways in which meanings are shaped (**AO2**).

Analysis: We have provided as much analysis (**AO2**) as possible, as well as exploring the significance and influence of contextual material (**AO3**) and different interpretations (**AO5**). It is a great idea to analyse the quotation in detail – you need to do more than just say what it means, but also try to explore a variety of different ways of interpreting it.

Use in essays on… Your answer needs to be focused to fulfil **AO1**. This section helps you choose relevant quotations and link them together for a stronger, more detailed essay.

How to use The Quotation Bank.

Many students spend time learning quotations by heart. This can be useful, but it is important to remember what you are meant to do with quotations once you get into the exam.

By using **The Quotation Bank**, not only will you have a huge number of textual, critical and contextual quotations to use in your essays, you will also have ideas on what to say about them, how to analyse them, how to link them together, and what questions to use them for.

These quotations can form the basis of your answer, making sure every point articulates an informed, personal response **(AO1)** and allows you to analyse ways in which meanings are shaped **(AO2)**.

The critical and contextual quotations allow you to easily and effectively explore the significance and influence of context **(AO3)**, and provide you with a variety of different readings to explore **(AO5).**

The textual quotations cover the whole text to allow you to show comprehensive whole text knowledge, and the critical and contextual quotations cover the full range of the text's publication history to help you explore the contexts in which the text was both written and received **(AO3)**.

Act One:
> HELMER: "Did you say bought? All those? Has my little songbird been spending all my money again?"

Interpretation: Ibsen establishes the paternalistic relationship between Helmer and Nora, with Helmer's character presented as patronisingly critical, a central idea in the play. The themes of misogyny, patriarchy and women's dependency on male earnings are key ones to consider.

Techniques: Language; Tone; Tri-colon.

Analysis:

- The tag question "Did you say bought?" establishes a patronising tone from Helmer, seemingly teasing his wife, but also subtly conveying incredulity and criticism of his wife's lack of control; Nora is portrayed as an extravagant wife who does not understand the value of money, reinforced by the use of "again".
- The triadic structure of three questions further reinforces this teasing criticism, one of Helmer's most explicit character traits, repeatedly infantilising Nora.
- The noun phrase (which may differ in each translation) used to label his wife presents Helmer's view of Nora as his ("my") possession and someone who is unwise and frivolous ("spending all") with money.

Use in essays on… Marriage; Gender; Patriarchy and Misogyny; Money and Work.

Act One:
> HELMER: "Just like a woman! But seriously, you know what I think. No borrowing. No debt. When a household relies on debt, it's slavery, it's vile. We've struggled this far without, the two of us – and we'll struggle on for a few more weeks, till we don't have to struggle anymore."

Interpretation: Ibsen depicts several key points which underpin the play's action: Helmer's criticism of borrowing and debt; his tenets for living appropriately and morally; and his attitude to the roles and behaviours of women.

Techniques: Motif; Foreshadowing; Repetition; Imperative.

Analysis:

- The exclamatory phrase, "Just like a woman!" emphasises Helmer's conventional understanding of women and their supposed inability to understand household economics, budgeting, and the significance of loans.
- Repetition of "no" reinforces Helmer's rigid belief that debt is wrong, depicting a dogmatic, paternalistic attitude to his household; connotations of "struggle" implies this is a moral journey, with any deviation seen as morally corrupt.
- The use of the inclusive "we" presents his view of his relationship with Nora, yet will prove ironic when Nora reveals the loan to Mrs Linde later in the play.

Use in essays on… Marriage; Gender; Money and Work; Truth and Deceit.

Act One:
MRS LINDE: "Wonderful, yes, to have all one needs." **NORA:** "Not just all one needs, but lots of money, lots."

Interpretation: This exchange indicates the connections between Nora and Mrs Linde: a shared desire for financial security; the foreshadowing of change in their social status associated with the role money plays in their lives; and the contrast in their personalities.

Techniques: Repetition; Language; Juxtaposition.

Analysis:
- Ibsen illustrates the difference between Mrs Linde, with her positive, content "Wonderful", juxtaposed with Nora's unsatisfied, discontented "not just".
- Symbolising the challenges faced by lower classes, "needs" implies necessity – Mrs Linde simply desires the basic requirements of life. Her use of "wonderful" has connotations of temperance rather than materialism; however, Mrs Linde's tone presents these "needs" as by no means certain in Norwegian society.
- Nora represents a middle-class wife whose financial "needs" appear to be met comfortably, in contrast to the working woman. Repetition of "lots" indicates Nora's greedy, material desires in contrast to Mrs Linde's temperance; it also alludes to her need to repay the loan from Krogstad.

Use in essays on… Money and Work; Society; Gender.

Act One:
> NORA: "Of course you have. And so do I. I've a right to be proud too."

Interpretation: Once again, Nora displays dominance over Mrs Linde in her self-centred desire to be the focus of their conversation. Is she inherently self-centred, or desperately seeking agency in a world where she is nothing more than a living "doll"?

Techniques: Sentence Structure; Tone.

Analysis:
- The use of "And so do I" redirects attention from Mrs Linde and refocuses it onto the self-centred Nora. She feels a need to impress and assert her own news rather than listening to her old friend, perhaps fighting against Helmer's incessant depiction of her as a caged bird.
- Nora's desire to equate herself with Mrs Linde's self-sufficiency further emphasises her limited world. Mrs Linde's actions to save her mother and two younger brothers are undoubtedly selfless and heroic; Ibsen suggests Norwegian society does not view Nora's action to save Helmer in the same light.
- There is a defiant yet somewhat desperate tone to Nora's statement of "I've a right to be proud too"; Ibsen suggests marriage deprives wives of the ability to feel pride, and we see the painful consequences of that.

Use in essays on… Marriage; Society; Money and Work.

Act One:
>   MRS LINDE: "A wife can't borrow without her husband's permission."

Interpretation: Nora's transgression is made explicit to the audience, thus emphasising the deceit that permeates the Helmer's marriage. Deceit and secrecy operate on a number of levels, from small daily acts (such as the hiding of the macaroons) to the significant self-deception at the heart of their relationship.

Techniques: Language; Sentence Structure; Motif; Foreshadowing.

Analysis:
- The clear, unequivocal language of "can't" alongside the declarative nature of the sentence stresses the significance of Nora's impetuous act and its illegality – even as an act designed to save her husband, it is still illegal.
- Mrs Linde is a vehicle for the revelation of Nora's fraudulent borrowing which is a canker in her marriage. It is important to note how quickly Nora confesses her past behaviours to Mrs Linde; does Ibsen present the secret as a burden weighing Nora down, or as an independent action in an otherwise caged life that Nora uses as a defiant rebuttal to Mrs Linde's claims Nora acts like "a child"?
- Mrs Linde's ongoing commentary on marriage is a catalyst for Nora's final act of defiance against Norwegian propriety; she refuses to seek "permission".

Use in essays on… Money and Work; Truth and Deceit; Patriarchy and Misogyny.

Act One:
> **NORA:** "It was exhausting. But it was thrilling too, to be sitting there working, earning money. Almost like a man."

Interpretation: Once again Ibsen underscores the complexity of Nora's behaviour and her later decision to leave, including her deception and self-deception; the need for her self-fulfilment; and her desire for purpose in her sterile, middle-class existence.

Techniques: Language; Juxtaposition.

Analysis:
- Within Nora's seemingly comfortable life, she must work like Mrs Linde to pay back her debt to Krogstad. She sees work as "thrilling" but does not have the self-awareness that, despite being "almost like a man", this is not a game.
- The work of men (Helmer and Krogstad) is valued and rewarded with "earning money"; women's domestic work is hidden and unpaid. We see Anne-Marie and Mrs Linde's caring responsibilities and the "exhausting" nature of them, and the immense personal sacrifices these two characters make in the name of work – their selflessness is juxtaposed with Nora's selfish actions later on.
- Nora works in secret; even in acts of agency designed to support her husband, deceit and dishonesty continue, reinforcing the broken nature of their marriage.

Use in essays on… Gender; Money and Work; Society; Truth and Deceit.

Act One:
DR RANK: "Most certainly. However dreadful I feel, I want to prolong the agony as long as possible. My patients all feel the same way. Not to mention those who are morally sick."

Interpretation: Dr Rank's character draws together a number of central themes, one of significance being the exploration of physical and metaphorical disease.

Techniques: Motif; Metaphor.

Analysis:
- Dr Rank suffers from an inherited disease, a consequence of his father's immoral behaviour. This physical disease is a metaphor for moral disease; Dr Rank's fragile spine could serve as a comment on the crumbling backbone of Nora and Helmer's marriage, or the weak underpinnings of Norwegian society.
- Ibsen uses the motif of sickness and disease to explore Norwegian social morals; while Dr Rank views Krogstad, who is blackmailing Nora, as "morally sick", we question Nora and Helmer's moral perspective.
- The intertwined existence of the characters is central to the denouement of the play; all wish to "prolong" their life, even in the face of immense hardship. Nora, Rank, Mrs Linde and Krogstad all face "dreadful" times, yet all fight on.

Use in essays on… Death and Disease; Society; Morality.

Act One:

> **MRS LINDE: "You don't need curing unless you're sick."**

Interpretation: Through Mrs Linde's opposition to Dr Rank's viewpoint, Ibsen's exploration of sickness is developed further. Moral corruption is presented by Helmer and Dr Rank as a disease; Mrs Linde focuses on providing a cure rather than on blame.

Techniques: Motif; Language.

Analysis:
- Mrs Linde acts as a commentator, challenging Dr Rank's moralistic judgement; in their discussion on society, Dr Rank represents a judgemental, condemnatory world view whilst Mrs Linde presents a caring, restorative society.
- Ibsen gives Mrs Linde prior experiences which enable her to challenge both Dr Rank and Nora's opinions and actions; as a female voice in the play, she is worldly and knowledgeable in contrast to the naïve and closeted Nora.
- Mrs Linde's supportive perspective provides redemption throughout the play – her mother dies free of burden; her brothers are able to "look after themselves"; and she provides Krogstad with the ability to "become a different person." In contrast, Helmer's belief in judgement, not redemption, forces Nora to leave.

Use in essays on… Society; Death and Disease; Morality.

Act One:
HELMER: "Darling, when I worked in the law I saw hardly anything else. Almost always, when people go bad young in life, the cause is a deceitful mother."

Interpretation: Helmer once again sets out his moral stance; Ibsen presents Helmer's narrow-minded and patriarchal viewpoints as stemming from institutions, constructs and social structures, rather than from any innately human perspective.

Techniques: Dramatic Irony; Hyperbole.

Analysis:

- Helmer's occupation in the "law" and as "manager of the bank" is key to the world of the play, giving him social status and, seemingly, the power to pass moral judgement. He uses "when I worked in the law" to imply a wisdom and gravitas before uttering the absurd suggestion that young people's poor decisions are "almost always" to be blamed on "a deceitful mother".
- Ibsen uses dramatic irony to underscore the deception within the marriage; Helmer does not realise he is condemning his own wife, heightening the absurdity of his proclamation. By laying the blame for adult behaviour solely on the mother, Ibsen reveals the misogynist social views that control Nora's behaviours and trap numerous women in Norwegian society.

Use in essays on… Patriarchy and Misogyny; Truth and Deceit; Money and Work.

Act Two:
   NORA: "He was bad. He's seriously ill. Lesions in the spine. Poor man. His father was horrible. Woman after woman. That's why the son…tainted blood…"

Interpretation: Nora explains Dr Rank's illness to Mrs Linde, clarifying the antecedent action for the audience so that we understand the Doctor's morose and morbid outlook.

Techniques: Language; Tone; Motif; Sentence Structure.

Analysis:
- Nora's use of "poor man" depicts her sympathy towards Dr Rank, reinforced by "seriously ill'" to describe his condition.
- Dr Rank's disease is symbolic of the immoral behaviour and secrecy that underpins the play. Here it is the father who is at fault, rather than the mother, but to what extent is Ibsen suggesting Nora's behaviour is a "lesion[s] in the spine" of her marriage which will create "tainted blood" in her children? Is she "horrible" in the same way Dr Rank's father is?
- Ibsen's choice of language, for instance "poor man", alongside the short sentence structure, creates a childish and patronising tone from Nora; her simplistic descriptions of Dr Rank to Mrs Linde imply she does not understand how worldly Mrs Linde is.

Use in essays on… Morality; Death and Disease.

Act Two:
MRS LINDE: "Nora, you are a child, sometimes. Listen to me. I'm older, more experienced."

Interpretation: Throughout Act Two Nora is exposed to the life experiences of the minor characters in the play, including Anne-Marie and Mrs Linde. Whether deliberately so or not, all characters convey lessons that have a role in shaping Nora's next steps.

Techniques: Language; Sentence Structure; Imperative; Juxtaposition.

Analysis:
- Despite the infantilising connotations of "you are a child" and the parental tone of "I'm older, more experienced", Mrs Linde is, unlike Helmer, seeking to support and protect Nora rather than force her to follow her suggestions.
- Helmer repeatedly insinuates that Nora is "a child", but he is determined for her to remain that way, as a doll for him to play with; Mrs Linde refers to Nora as "a child" but with the aim of elevating her successfully into the adult world.
- "Listen to me" may be an imperative, with Mrs Linde seemingly exerting power over Nora, but it treats Nora with dignity in receiving the wisdom Mrs Linde is seeking to impart; the tone of "listen to me" is caring and concerned, treating Nora with respect, rather than the belittling approach of Helmer.

Use in essays on… Morality; Relationships; Truth and Deceit; Society.

Act Two:

> **NORA: "I'd play fairies, dance in the moonlight. Torvald."**

Interpretation: Ibsen presents Nora as trying to enthral Helmer by playing a part; whilst modern audiences may focus on the societal roles Nora has forced upon her by Helmer, and the injustice of this, Ibsen also explores the exploitation of roleplaying by Nora herself.

Techniques: Motif; Imagery; Tone.

Analysis:
- Nora tries to manipulate Helmer through playing a character; note here she is a magical fairy with an ethereal nature, something bewitching but also unreal.
- Nora will also "play" a role when she dances the Tarantella; these roles allude to the performative nature of her relationship with Helmer, and Act Two also begins with "fancy dress". Indeed, her performative roles in Act Two and Three are designed to stop Helmer discovering the truth sitting in his post box.
- This conscious choice signifies the lack of reality in their relationship and their reliance on playing roles. Whether a "little squirrel", "little bird" or a "fair[y]", the role Nora plays is always fictional and not based on any human character.

Use in essays on… Appearance and Reality; Marriage; Relationships; Truth and Deceit.

Act Two:
   HELMER: "Darling, I don't blame you for being upset, even though it's so insulting to me. That's right, insulting. To think that I'd be afraid of that…that worn-out pen-pusher. I don't blame you because it shows how much you love me."

Interpretation: Helmer unwittingly reveals his patriarchal and patronising relationship with Nora; whilst his tone and use of "Darling" implies he believes he is being fair and just, modern audiences in particular would question his perspective on the situation.

Techniques: Repetition; Language; Foreshadowing.

Analysis:
- Helmer takes a paternalistic and egotistical role here; he places himself in a position of power through the repetition of "I don't blame you".
- He emphasises his superior position in society through aggressive, assertive language, referring to Krogstad with the insult "worn-out pen-pusher" and repeating the accusation that Nora is "insulting" him. At the end of the play, the speed with which he breaks down implies this masculine bravado is just an act.
- His confidence in "how much you [Nora] love me" is misplaced and foreshadows her realisation that this "love" no longer exists because he is, ultimately, unable to forgive.

Use in essays on… Appearance and Reality; Marriage; Relationships; Truth and Deceit.

Act Two:
DR RANK: "I swore I'd tell you before I…went. Now. Nora, now you know. And you know that you can rely on me, as on no one else."

Interpretation: Dr Rank and Nora are now bound by his confession; her fantasy of a benefactor has been complicated by Rank's additional declaration of his feelings for Nora, with the reality of love and death interfering with her intentions.

Techniques: Repetition; Irony; Language.

Analysis:

- Dr Rank prepares Nora for his death, with the theme of morbidity made more explicit here. This proclamation links with the cross on the card he will leave in the letterbox; in both cases Rank chooses truth over self-deception, presented in the frankness with which he deals with his impending death ("before I…went") and the clear, unequivocal acceptance of the truth of his condition symbolised by the black cross.
- Despite connotations of truth and honesty in language such as "swore", "tell you" and "know", it is ironic that Rank develops their relationship further by binding them together through another secret – that of his love for her.
- Nora now knows it is untenable to ask Rank to pay off her debt as a "favour".

Use in essays on… Death and Disease; Relationships; Appearance and Reality.

Act Two:
KROGSTAD: "Your husband cares so little for you? He knows the harm I can do you, and still he –"

Interpretation: Krogstad is perceptive, addressing Helmer's lack of courage and exposing the significant weakness in their relationship. Ibsen presents Helmer as a man who is certainly unable to provide the "miracle" Nora later dreams of.

Techniques: Repetition; Foreshadowing.

Analysis:

- Krogstad's question is incisive, and "still he" is scornful of Helmer's masculinity; indeed, is this the moment in the play Nora realises she needs a "miracle" that will never come?
- The repetition of "you" emphasises Nora's isolation in the play, and foreshadows Helmer's selfish reaction later on – Krogstad's question is proven to be a factual statement as Helmer does indeed "care[s] so little for you" and instead focuses exclusively on himself and the societal consequences.
- Krogstad maintains his threat of exposure and social disgrace in order to continue his blackmail; the use of "harm" has connotations of aggression and violence, but both characters know it is social disgrace that would cause "harm".

Use in essays on… Money and Work; Truth and Deceit; Relationships; Marriage.

Act Two:
  HELMER: *"Nora, darling, anyone'd think your life depended on this dance."*

Interpretation: Helmer unwittingly exposes the truth of Nora's dance, but Ibsen presents an uncertainty – is the dance one of desperation and fear that an old life might slip away, or a dance of freedom celebrating a new life yet to come?

Techniques: Dramatic Irony; Language; Staging.

Analysis:
- The Tarantella is highly performative, reinforcing a focus on appearance within the relationship. Whilst the dance is one of possession, symbolising the sexual desire Helmer feels for Nora, it is ironic that he focuses on Nora's technical dancing ability rather than fulfil his role in the flirtatious, sexual performance.
- Dramatic irony in "life depended" reinforces Helmer's ignorance, and focuses on the "life" Nora chooses; in some way, Nora has more agency than ever here.
- The accompanying stage directions suggest she dances "ever more wildly", that "her hair falls over her shoulder", "pays no attention" and "is engrossed". Is Ibsen depicting a woman dancing out of fear and despair, desperately trying to save her old life; or is this a woman finally free of societal shackles, dancing with a joyous abandon and experiencing what an independent life may bring?

Use in essays on… Appearance and Reality; Truth and Deceit.

Act Three:

> MRS LINDE: "Now I'm alone…empty, thrown away. Where's the satisfaction in working for oneself? Nils, give me someone, something to work for."

Interpretation: Whilst Nora is on a path to independence, Mrs Linde seeks dependence and partnership; Ibsen presents the autonomy both women have in making these decisions, despite the very different outcomes.

Techniques: Foreshadowing; Imagery.

Analysis:
- Whilst "I'm alone" foreshadows Nora's future, Mrs Linde was "empty, thrown away", thus used and discarded by society. In contrast, Nora "takes the case" at the end of the play – it is her choice to leave, rather than being "thrown away".
- Ibsen depicts dignity and honour in work, with Mrs Linde repeating the idea of work as satisfying, echoing Nora's positive depictions of it earlier in the play.
- Mrs Linde desires a relationship where she can be a care-giver. "Someone, something" gives her a sense of purpose, unlike the caged Nora; even Nora's children are cared for predominantly by Anne-Marie rather than Nora.
- The past intruding on the present is more positive here; rather than hereditary sufferings of Dr Rank and Nora, here it is a chance for a mutual new beginning.

Use in essays on… Relationships; Marriage; Society.

Act Three:
> MRS LINDE: "Helmer must know the truth. The secret must come out. No more lies, tricks, they must understand each other."

Interpretation: Mrs Linde directly addresses the falsity withing the Helmer marriage and her imperative tone reinforces the certainty of her views; as an observer throughout the play, she comprehends the solution, unlike Nora and Helmer, who are blind to the truth.

Techniques: Imperative; Repetition; Language.

Analysis:

- Mrs Linde's moral viewpoint is clear; there can be no secrets in a relationship, reinforced by the repetition of "must". However, whilst she begins with a focus on Helmer, she grasps the fact "they must understand each other" – she is not espousing rigid societal views, but rather genuine concern for individuals.
- Ibsen presents Mrs Linde and Krogstad in juxtaposition to the Helmers; Linde and Krogstad enter their relationship with a full knowledge of each other's pasts and "secrets", with the result being "the luckiest day of my [Krogstad's] life".
- Language associated with deceit throughout the play is often euphemistic, such as "songbird" or "squirrel". Here, Mrs Linde's language is unequivocal; the appearances in the marriage are actually "secret[s]…lies, tricks".

Use in essays on… Relationships; Marriage; Truth and Deceit; Appearance and Reality.

Act Three:
DR RANK: "Why shouldn't we enjoy every blessed thing? As much as we can, as long as we can."

Interpretation: Ibsen uses the dramatic irony of Dr Rank's situation to pose a question, not to Helmer, but to the audience – are the restrictive, conformist societal structures of Norwegian life denying people the ability to "enjoy every blessed thing?"

Techniques: Foreshadowing; Language; Dramatic Irony.

Analysis:

- In a play where so many characters focus almost exclusively on "I", Dr Rank frames his question with the collective "we", allowing Ibsen to suggest enjoyment and pleasure should be accessible to all in society.
- "Blessed" has spiritual connotations, implying that seeking enjoyment from life is a religious imperative; however, it contrasts with the indulgent, excessive tone of "as much as we can, as long as we can", conveying a human, bodily indulgence.
- Dr Rank's rhetorical question foreshadows Nora's decision later on. Nora and Rank's final interaction sees her light a match before Rank utters, "Sleep well. And thanks for the light", a symbol of the epiphany both Rank and Nora have.

Use in essays on… Death and Disease; Morality; Society.

Act Three:
> HELMER: "You have to come to terms. Do you understand what you've done? Do you understand?"

Interpretation: Helmer demonstrates his anger and disgust at the revelation in the letter; Ibsen presents him as valuing his social status above his marriage to Nora.

Techniques: Repetition; Imperative.

Analysis:

- Helmer's desperation and desire to save himself is expressed through questions and imperatives, and he resorts to legalistic language ("come to terms") rather than a more human, emotional response.
- His anger depicts the superficial nature of his relationship with Nora; his love is dependent on Nora being a doll in the "Doll's House" he has constructed, and the repetition of "you" emphasises the lack of unity within their relationship.
- Helmer's weak character is exposed; he is limited by a warped moral code that is less about genuine morality and more about the social code of the middle class.
- Ironically, he places focus on trying to "understand" the social consequences of Nora's behaviour, oblivious to her impending actions, whereas Nora's response ("Now, I understand") depicts inner clarity and personal understanding.

Use in essays on… Morality; Marriage; Truth and Deceit.

Act Three:
> HELMER: "To wake up to this! Eight years…my joy, my life, my wife…Lies, deceit…a criminal. No way out. No end."

Interpretation: Krogstad earlier accused Mrs Linde of "female hysteria"; in this scene it is Helmer who responds hysterically. When truth is revealed in the play, it is men who fall apart whilst women remain rational, providing solutions and courage of conviction.

Techniques: Metaphor; Tri-colon; Repetition; Sentence Structure; Hyperbole.

Analysis:

- Ibsen uses the metaphor of sleep to convey Helmer's shock at Nora's revelation, implying Norwegian society is asleep to the consequences of its societal structures; the fractured sentence structure mimics the fractured nature of their relationship, and the ease with which social constructs can collapse.
- Repetition of "my" conveys Helmer's possessive, paternalistic nature towards Nora; the structure of the sentence means "my wife" comes as an afterthought, and it is not clear if "my joy, my life" are in any way associated with "my wife".
- Helmer's disdain is expressed through cruel accusations ("a criminal"). Nora's hopes of "a miracle" are crushed; indeed, since Helmer sees "no way out", it is left to Nora to "set [him] free".

Use in essays on… Marriage; Truth and Deceit; Patriarchy and Misogyny.

Act Three:
   HELMER: "You've killed my happiness. You've destroyed my future. I'm trapped, in his claws. No mercy. He'll do whatever he likes to me, demand, insist, I can't refuse. No way out. A silly, empty-headed woman – and now I'm dead."

Interpretation: One misogynistic argument against contemporary women's rights was the allegedly fragile, overly-emotional nature of female personalities; Ibsen subverts this idea at the play's conclusion, depicting Helmer as hysterical, theatrical and over-wrought.

Techniques: Sentence Structure; Hyperbole; Irony; Imagery.

Analysis:

- In Act Three, Mrs Linde and Nora speak with clarity and concision; their sentences are dynamic and powerful. In contrast, Helmer and Krogstad talk in confused utterances, their speech mimicking their lack of understanding.
- Helmer's hyperbolic imagery of being "killed", "destroyed" and "trapped, in his claws" is pathetic; alongside his assertion Krogstad will "demand, insist, I can't refuse", and "I'm dead", Helmer is not an image of strong, masculine control.
- "Killed my happiness", "destroyed my future", "I'm trapped" and "no way out" are deeply ironic – Helmer, and Norwegian society, show "no mercy" to Nora and the contemporary women for who these scenarios were actually true.

Use in essays on…Gender; Patriarchy and Misogyny; Appearance and Reality.

Act Three:
> **NORA:** "When I lived with Daddy, he told me his views on everything, so I shared his views. If I disagreed I didn't say so: he'd have hated it. He called me his little dolly-baby, and played with me as I played with my dollies."

Interpretation: Ibsen depicts Nora's awakening to the truth of her situation. She considers how her father controlled her thinking; Ibsen traces her relationship with Helmer along a path women have to follow, from one man's rules to another.

Techniques: Motif; Repetition; Metaphor.

Analysis:
- "He told me" stresses the didactic nature of the society in which Nora grew up, and "I didn't say so" and "he'd have hated it" have dark undertones – Ibsen presents no room for dissent in Norwegian society.
- "I lived with Daddy" seems cold and distant; it does not convey a close, loving connection between father and daughter, with "his little dolly-baby", "dollies" and the repetition of "played" all suggesting an objectified, possessive relationship between them.
- Much like Dr Rank's inherited condition or Nora's inherited traits, a patriarchal, misogynistic control of women is transferred from the father to the husband.

Use in essays on… Patriarchy and Misogyny; Marriage; Truth and Deceit; Gender.

Act Three:

> NORA: "It was the truth. I can't bring them up. I've someone else to bring up first – myself. You can't help. I must do it myself. That's why I'm leaving you."

Interpretation: Despite enraged reactions from some contemporary audiences to Nora's decision, Ibsen does not portray her as a stereotypical, hysterical cliche; instead, he depicts a calm, rational woman making independent, logical decisions about her own life.

Techniques: Sentence Structure; Language; Repetition.

Analysis:

- Repetition of "bring up" is not a sign of abandonment; rather, Ibsen presents Nora as breaking the cycle of hereditary control, giving herself and her children the potential for a future decided by themselves rather than parental influence.
- Repetition of "I", "I've" and "I'm" caused many contemporary audiences to view Nora in a selfish, self-centred light. However, Ibsen depicts Nora ending the play by asserting her rights as an individual, defined first and foremost as "myself" rather than as a wife or mother.
- The short, definitive sentences reinforced by the forceful tone of "can't", "must" and "that's why" present Nora's clarity of thought; she is a rational, coherent women in response to Helmer's chaotic ramblings.

Use in essays on… Gender; Truth and Deceit; Morality; Society; Relationships.

Act Three:

STAGE DIRECTION: *"A door slams, off."*

Interpretation: Nora's exit was originally viewed as selfish, cowardly and unfeminine by many in the audience. Perhaps the subsequent outrage was because Nora allows no reply; it is an unequivocal, finite action that societal structures around her cannot stop and, just like Helmer, the audience are powerless against Nora's decision.

Techniques: Staging; Irony.

Analysis:
- Whilst Rank shuts himself away to die, this shut door ironically symbolises new openings for Nora – the closed door is a beginning of a new chapter in her life.
- Although outraging some contemporary audiences, Nora's decision is a strong, defiant and powerful action that gives her full control; it contrasts with Krogstad's weak, corrupt blackmailing, or Helmer's hysterical reactions.
- Earlier, Mrs Linde tells Krogstad, "What else could I do? I had to break with you. It was essential to kill everything you felt for me." She is seen as bold and compassionate. Nora's decision mirrors this; since Ibsen gives Mrs Linde the happy ending she deserves, can we presume this is still an option for Nora?

Use in essays on… Morality; Society; Gender.

In a letter to Hegel, Ibsen (1878) spoke of working on, "a play of modern life."

Interpretation: In terms of Ibsen's playwriting career, *A Doll's House* signified a change from the poetic plays of his earlier work to a desire to reveal truths about society.

Analysis:

- The audience may question what aspects of "modern life" are being explored. The play begins with what appears to be a conventional middle-class marriage; the action itself is seemingly mundane; and the marriage roles follow social norms (a working father and a housewife with children cared for by a nanny).
- As the play develops, Ibsen's observations on the conventions of Norwegian society become a series of strictures about its stultifying nature, challenging a contemporary audience's preconceptions.
- It is "a play of modern life", but whilst contemporary audiences may have recognised the roles and societal structures on stage, and perhaps within themselves, they didn't necessarily recognise Ibsen's conclusions; indeed, many were supposedly outraged by Nora's final act. It is important to discuss whether this outrage was a genuine reaction; one moulded by societal expectations; or shaped by an uncomfortable recognition of themselves in characters on stage.

Use in essays on…Society; Gender.

In his notes on *A Doll's House*, Ibsen (1878) declares,
"A woman cannot be herself in contemporary society, it is an exclusively male society with laws drafted by men, and with counsel and judges who judge feminine conduct from the male point of view."

Interpretation: Gail Finney argues that, despite Ibsen's protestations he is not a feminist and that, "I am not a member of the Women's Rights League", his work was "enthusiastically welcomed by feminist thinkers in Norway and throughout Europe."

Analysis:

- "Cannot be herself" and "judge" suggest Ibsen is warning of what will happen when "women in general woke up to the injustices that had been committed against them" (Finney). This awakening is inevitable; Ibsen imbues Nora with the courage to close the door on "contemporary society" and "be herself."
- Nora herself evolves to realise she is judged by all the men in the play, and that she must "think things out" on her own terms; she learns, as the audience must, that the law is, "not what I always thought it was, and I can't believe it's right."
- Ibsen presents rational "counsel" and "conduct" from Anne-Marie and Mrs Linde, in contrast to the underhand blackmail of Krogstad, the morbid marking of his own death by Dr Rank, and the pitiful behaviour of Helmer.

Use in essays on… Marriage; Gender; Patriarchy and Misogyny; Society.

> Ibsen (1878) also explores the position of motherhood in society, stating it is like, "certain insects who go away and die when she has done her duty in the propagation of the race."

Interpretation: Nora has two roles in her family: wife and mother. Helmer is judgemental about both of these, and Nora concludes she is not fit to educate her children since she needs to educate herself first.

Analysis:
- Ibsen sees women as reduced to specific roles in his society; as Helmer declares, "you're a wife, a mother. They come first." Nora challenges this ("I don't think so"), but Ibsen is not entirely dismissive of the value of these roles; Kristine Linde needs to find security in life and seeks this in the role of wife and care giver. It is not the specific roles Ibsen criticises; it is the lack of personal choice.
- For Mrs Linde perhaps "anguish and fear" have returned and she does not want to bear them alone; "go away and die" emphasises the loneliness and isolation women could face in Norwegian society.
- Nora, however, as a "human being" rather than "certain insects", does not want to "go away and die"; indeed, she wants to live and not sacrifice her own life for love, seeing her "duty" to herself, not to the "propagation of the race".

Use in essays on… Marriage; Society; Gender; Relationships; Death and Disease.

Peter Watts (1965) highlights the fact that,

> "To nineteenth-century Europe, the idea of a woman not only forsaking her marriage vows, but also displaying a mind of her own and renouncing her duty of unquestioning obedience to her husband, was almost indecent; that she should also make him look small was scandalous."

Interpretation: Ibsen's desire to "revel in adverse criticism" is apparent here. He scandalises Norwegian society through his stark revelations of what can happen behind the closed door of a marriage.

Analysis:

- Ibsen's Nora grows significantly from the start of the play; however, we see her small acts of rebellion are already in place, claiming, "you told me not to" when she secretly eats macaroons, her only respite from "vows" and "duty".
- Nora quietly renounces what Watts describes as her "unquestioning obedience", which Ibsen builds throughout the play into an ending so dramatic he was forced to rewrite it; he saw the rewriting as a "barbarous act of violence".
- Helmer's reaction at the end of the play conveys the reaction of a contemporary male and ultimately justifies Nora's actions. It could be argued Watts is incorrect that Nora makes Helmer "look small"; it is the behaviour of Helmer himself, and the Norwegian society that empowers him, that makes him "look small".

Use in essays on… Society; Gender; Marriage; Truth and Deceit.

Referring to a "conservative, stagnant society", Bjorn Hemmer (1994) argues that within many of Ibsen's plays,
"…it is precisely the defenders of this society who are presented as the least free."

Interpretation: Helmer defends his status and roles within society at the end of the play, roles he is prepared to hold on to at any price. He wants to be a "pillar of society" but, in remaining so, loses Nora.

Analysis:
- Ibsen uses *A Doll's House* to challenge Norwegian societal desire for bourgeoise living; the audience go through the door into the private sphere to see the difference between "official and the private life of the bourgeoise individual".
- The audience are presented with the deception necessary to maintain the bourgeoise lifestyle of the Helmers; indeed, the "defenders of this society" are surrounded by fancy-dress, performative dances and blackmail.
- Ibsen presents a challenge to family as the central institution of society, instead focusing on the needs of the individual - Nora. He examines how a "latent crisis suddenly becomes visible" which destabilises the Helmer household and reveals to Helmer that he is a victim of his beliefs; Nora shuts one door whilst opening another to a new world, whilst Helmer remains trapped and "the least free".

Use in essays on…Marriage; Society; Gender; Appearance and Reality.

Hemmer (1994) also places focus on Ibsen's multi-faceted presentation of women in the play, reminding us that,

> "in the shadow of Nora one can find the self-effacing Kristine Linde, who sees life's meaning exclusively in terms of service to others. This two-sided ideal of woman is to be found in all phases of Ibsen's authorship."

Interpretation: Nora's need for freedom contrasts Mrs Linde's. Mrs Linde states that she needs somebody to live for – Krogstad. She gains security through her relationship with Krogstad, which is just as liberating to Mrs Linde as Nora's exit is to her.

Analysis:

- Mrs Linde has learnt, through experience of struggle and loneliness, the value of truth. This is the gift she gives to the Helmers, and the one that sets Nora free.
- Dramatically, as Mrs Linde negotiates her relationship with Krogstad, the Helmers' marriage unravels, a necessary act for the realisation of truth. Through Mrs Linde, Ibsen presents a woman who forges her own path to find "life's meaning", and who is rewarded with the ending she desires.
- Whilst Hemmer sees Mrs Linde as self-effacing, she is quietly determined to act as a truth-bringer; though she desires to be a wife and mother, these seem to be her sincere wishes, her own "ideal" – they are not forced on her by society.

Use in essays on… Marriage; Society; Gender; Truth and Deceit.

Finally, Hemmer (1994) discusses the dramatic structure of the play, claiming, "Nora's situation illustrates the pattern central to Ibsen's realistic problem dramas: the individual in opposition to a hostile society. The structure…is simple – and nobody can be in any doubt as to where the author's sympathies lie."

Interpretation: Nora is the character in opposition to her "hostile society". She challenges the core beliefs of both her husband and her friend, yet her truth is "individual and subjective"; she has to go out into the world alone to find out who she really is, to reassess her values and her beliefs.

Analysis:

- Ibsen creates his new type of drama, "the realistic problem drama", in response to Eugene Scribe's popular "well-made play". Ibsen uses similar devices to Scribe, such as coincidence and revelations, which heighten an audience's anticipation, but we come to a "realistic" ending, not a happy one: there is no "miracle"; the letter is opened; Helmer does not relent; and Nora leaves.
- When an "individual" is in conflict with "society", it is often the individual at fault, and on first viewing Nora is certainly flawed; yet, as the play continues, Hemmer is correct that there is no "doubt as to where the author's sympathies lie", even if these sympathies contradict those of many contemporary audiences.

Use in essays on… Society; Truth and Deceit; Patriarchy and Misogyny.

Playwright Arthur Miller (1994) also discusses Ibsen's focus on reality and moral debate, perhaps taking inspiration for his own work, stating,

"Ibsenism – also imagines itself to be a revolt against the well-made play, quite as though Ibsen was not himself the first to attack that kind of play. Instead of being well-made his plays are true… they follow the psycho-moral dilemma, not the plot."

Interpretation: One could argue the plot of *A Doll's House* is clear but somewhat mundane; it is the psychological and moral problems in the play that provide the drama. Each character has a "psycho-moral dilemma" to engage with, but Nora and Mrs Linde's inner psychologies are the richer, complex and more engaging ones.

Analysis:

- Mrs Linde understands both Krogstad's and Nora's "psycho-moral dilemma" and is pivotal in both; she understands their psychological needs, and amongst an audience with little appetite for subversive thinking, acts as a tool for Ibsen to articulate a "revolt" or "attack" on conventional societal thought. Whilst Mrs Linde is traditional in her choices, she is open-minded and worldly.
- Nora's "psycho-moral dilemma" is central to "Ibsenism": to reject what her society believes and to leave behind her children in order to find truth. There is an affinity between Ibsen and Nora; it would be easier for both to follow "the plot" and stick to the "well-made play", but they choose to "revolt" instead.

Use in essays on… Truth and Deceit; Appearance and Reality; Society.

Gail Finney (1994) makes clear that,
> "It is no accident that Ibsen's most famous emancipated woman character achieves self-realisation by turning her back on her husband and children…in order to reach genuine maturity she must leave this life behind."

Interpretation: Nora must confront and come to terms with her situation in her "Doll's House". She realises that has gone from being "Daddy's dolly-baby" to a home which has been nothing but a "Wendy house" – the only escape is to "leave this life behind."

Analysis:
- Part of the emancipation comes through Mrs Linde, who is at first someone to show off to but then someone to confide in; she does not allow Nora to live for the miraculous, and is part of her means of growth. Although Finney suggests a "self-realisation", it involves other women in the play as catalysts for change.
- The audience become aware of the superficiality of Nora's role as wife, with the hints of deceit and rebelliousness, the use of fancy-dress, and the language of role-play permeating the play; there is nothing "genuine" about it.
- The revelation of the forged signature shows us what Nora could truly be if she decides to leave; the "maturity" Finney describes was evident in Nora's description of "sitting there working, earning money" earlier in the play.

Use in essays on… Gender; Truth and Deceit; Marriage; Society; Relationships.

> Simon Williams (1994) explores difficulties an actor may face in the play, stating, "perhaps the most formidable challenge faced by the Ibsen actor was the questionable moral quality of his characters, which could easily alienate them from the audience."

Interpretation: Whilst we sympathise with Nora's situation, we may not always sympathise with Nora's character. Ibsen deliberately depicts her, and all his characters, as flawed, and Williams is correct that they could "easily alienate" an audience.

Analysis:
- Continuing Hemmer's exploration of the realistic nature of Ibsen's work, we are not presented with simplistic characters or situations; they are of "questionable moral quality", be they blackmailers, unrequited lovers, or hypocrites.
- All characters have unpleasant traits (even Nora's reaction to Mrs Linde's arrival is entirely self-centred, again doing nothing to endear her to an audience), but Williams is correct in his use of "questionable". To what extent is it Nora's fault she is spoilt? Does Krogstad have no choice but to blackmail Nora? We question whether the individual is at fault, or the society that shapes them.
- Nora's true self is revealed slowly – our hostility fades as we see she is trapped in the role of an immature child, forced to play such a "questionable" character.

Use in essays on… Marriage; Gender; Morality.

Performance History

One aspect of *A Doll's House* performance history is in understanding time and place, differentiating between, for instance, early-1880s Norway, late-1880s London, or Paris of the mid-1890s. Whilst many were outraged by the play, much of this outrage came from conservative critics. Despite, or perhaps because of this outrage, the play was successful across Europe, striking a nerve with sections of society seeking change. Importantly, Ibsen famously re-wrote the ending to stop others from doing so first, not because audiences disliked it. Notably, Hedwig Niemann-Raabe, who triggered the rewriting by refusing to perform the original ending, was disgusted not at Nora leaving Helmer, but at her abandoning her children; motherly rejection seemed to shake audiences more than Nora's exit as a wife. Just as important, however, was the restoration of the original ending due, in no small part, to audience demand.

The nature of translation, alongside variation in societal tastes, led to many rewritings. In London in 1884, audiences were presented with *Breaking a Butterfly*, an adaptation restoring a happy home and social convention. It is vital to question rewritings that present 'happy' endings: are these because audiences could not recognise Nora's behaviour as fathomable; because we demand a 'happy' ending when attending the theatre; or because certain facets of society want to restore power structures? Socio-political landscapes could explain *Breaking a Butterfly*; English audiences of 1879 were not in a place to accept Nora, but a fin de siècle mood of change made *A Doll's House* a great success in late 1880s London.

Performance history can also explore dramatic convention. *A Doll's House* brings no resolution or closure; Ibsen's realism was thematically though-provoking but also subverted the idea of what drama was for. As Miller asserts, the play does not focus on being "well-made", and Williams is correct that characters "could easily alienate…the audience." To this end, directors have many choices in what they want the final message of a production to be; with morally dubious characters and no ending to speak of, the concluding 'message' of the play, if there must be one, is more open to dramatic interpretation than most plays offer.

How to revise effectively.

One mistake people often make is to try to revise EVERYTHING!

This is clearly not possible.

Instead, once you understand the text in detail, a good idea is to pick five or six major themes, and four or five major characters, and revise these in great detail. The same is true when exploring key scenes – you are unlikely to be able to closely analyse every single line, so focus on the *skills* of analysis and interpretation and then be ready for any question, rather than covering the whole text and trying to pre-prepare everything.

If, for example, you revised Marriage and Morality, you will also have covered a huge amount of material to use in questions about Gender, Truth and Deceit, and Society.

It is also sensible to avoid revising quotations in isolation; instead, bring together two or three textual quotations as well as a critical and contextual quotation so that any argument you make is supported and explored in detail.

Finally, make sure material is pertinent to the questions you will be set. By revising the skills of interpretation and analysis you will be able to answer the actual question set in the exam, rather than the one you wanted to come up.

Suggested Revision Activities

A great cover and repeat exercise – Cover the whole page, apart from the quotation at the top. Can you now fill in the four sections without looking – Interpretations, Techniques, Analysis, Use in essays on…?

This also works really well as **a revision activity with a friend** – cover the whole page, apart from the quotation at the top. If you read out the quotation, can they tell you the four sections without looking – Interpretations, Techniques, Analysis, Use in essays on…?

For both activities, could you extend the analysis and interpretation further, or provide an alternative interpretation? Also, can you find another quotation that extends or counters the point you have just made?

Your very own Quotation Bank! Using the same headings and format as The Quotation Bank, find 10 more quotations from throughout the text (select them from many different sections of the text to help develop whole text knowledge) and create your own revision cards.

Essay writing – They aren't always fun, but writing essays is great revision. Devise a practice question and try taking three quotations and writing out a perfect paragraph, making sure you add connectives, technical vocabulary and sophisticated language.

Glossary

Dramatic Irony – When the audience knows something the characters don't: Ibsen uses the dramatic irony of Rank's situation to pose a question not to Helmer, but to the audience – are the restrictive, conformist societal structures of Norwegian life denying people the ability to "enjoy every blessed thing?"

Foreshadowing – When the writer alludes to or makes reference to something that is yet to come in the text: Helmer's confidence in "how much you [Nora] love me" is misplaced and foreshadows her realisation that this "love" no longer exists.

Hyperbole – An exaggerated statement that intensifies or adds emphasis: Helmer's hyperbolic imagery of being "killed", "destroyed" and "trapped, in his claws" is pathetic.

Imagery – Figurative language that appeals to the senses of the audience: Mrs Linde was "empty, thrown away", thus used and discarded by society. In contrast, Nora "takes the case" at the end of the play – it is her choice to leave, rather than being "thrown away".

Imperative – A sentence that gives a command or an order: "Listen to me" may be an imperative, with Mrs Linde seemingly exerting power over Nora, but it treats Nora with dignity in receiving the wisdom Mrs Linde is seeking to impart.

Irony – A statement that suggests one thing but often has a contrary meaning: despite connotations of truth and honesty in language such as "swore", "tell you" and "know", it is ironic that Rank develops their relationship further by binding them together through another secret.

Juxtaposition – Two ideas, images or words placed next to each other to create a contrasting effect: Ibsen illustrates the difference between Mrs Linde, with her positive, content "wonderful", juxtaposed with Nora's unsatisfied, discontented "not just".

Language – The vocabulary chosen to create effect.

Metaphor – A word or phrase used to describe something else so that the first idea takes on the associations of the second: Ibsen uses the metaphor of sleep ("to wake up to this") to convey Helmer's shock at Nora's revelation, implying Norwegian society is asleep to the consequences of its societal structures.

Motif – A significant idea, element or symbol repeated throughout the text: Ibsen uses the motif of sickness and disease to explore Norwegian social morals.

Repetition – When a word, phrase or idea is repeated to reinforce it: repetition of "no" reinforces Helmer's rigid belief that debt is wrong.

Sentence Structure – The way the writer has ordered the words in a sentence to create a certain effect: Helmer's fractured sentence structure mimics the fractured nature of their relationship.

Staging – Directions given to the director or actor to aid interpretation: the shut door ironically symbolises new openings for Nora – the closed door is a beginning of a new chapter in her life.

Tone – The mood or atmosphere created by the writer: "Did you say bought?" establishes a patronising tone from Helmer.

Tri-colon – A list of three words or phrases for effect: the triadic structure of three questions further reinforces this teasing criticism, one of Helmer's most explicit character traits, repeatedly infantilising Nora.

Acknowledgments:

H Ibsen: taken from *The Oxford Ibsen Volume V. Pillars of Society, A Doll's House, Ghosts*, edited and translated by J McFarlane, published by Oxford University Press, 1961.

P Watts: *Introduction* from *A Doll's House and Other Plays*, published by Penguin Books, 1965.

B Hemmer: *Ibsen and the realistic problem drama*, from *The Cambridge Companion to Ibsen*, edited by J McFarlane, published by Cambridge University Press, 1994.

A Miller: *Ibsen and the drama of today*, from *The Cambridge Companion to Ibsen*, edited by J McFarlane, published by Cambridge University Press, 1994.

G Finney: *Ibsen and feminism*, from *The Cambridge Companion to Ibsen*, edited by J McFarlane, published by Cambridge University Press, 1994.

S Williams: *Ibsen and the theatre 1877-1900*, from *The Cambridge Companion to Ibsen*, edited by J McFarlane, published by Cambridge University Press, 1994.

A note on translation: As we are dealing with quotations from *A Doll's House* in translation, we have taken all quotations from the Cambridge Literature edition, translated by Kenneth McLeish, edited by Mary Rafferty, published by Cambridge University Press, 1995. The quotations we have used may differ from the edition you use in your studies, but the interpretation, analysis and discussion remain just as pertinent.